ALPHABET
of
MOVEMENTS
of
THE HUMAN BODY

ALPHABET
OF
MOVEMENTS
OF
THE HUMAN BODY

A study in recording the movements of the human body by means of musical signs

by

V. I. STEPANOV

Artist of the Imperial Theatres of Saint Petersburg

Translated by Raymond Lister from the French Edition of 1892

Noverre Press

First published in 1958
This edition published in 2019 by
The Noverre Press
Southwold House
Isington Road
Binsted
Hampshire
GU34 4PH

© 2019 The Noverre Press

ISBN 978-1-906830-83-0

CONTENTS

Translator's Preface	1
Bibliographical Note	3
Report of the Commission of the Imperial Ballet Company of Saint Petersburg	5
Introduction	7
Anatomical Notes	11
Chapter I. Notes and Signs	16
Chapter II. Leg Movements	18
Chapter III. Arm Movements	23
Chapter IV. Movements of the Torso (with Notes on Circular Movements and Signs of Increase and Decrease)	27
Chapter V. Duration and Arrangement of the Notes	30
Chapter VI. Turns of the Body	33
Chapter VII. Gymnastics	34
Chapter VIII. Choreography	36
Key to the Anatomical Illustrations	40
Notes	41
Appendix I	43
Appendix II	45
Appendix III	46
Acknowledgements	47

Dedicated

to

The Imperial Theatre School

of

Saint Petersburg

TRANSLATOR'S PREFACE

THE problem of recording movements of the human body is almost as old as the art of dancing. It has been said that the ancient Egyptians had a system of notation, but there is no real evidence to prove that this was so.

To-day, when there is more general interest in the subject than ever before, there are several systems in use—one of them is described in this book—and serious attempts are being made to put them into practice, both for recording ballets and for such things as research in industrial welfare[1].

The most scientific system of all is that variously known as Kinetographie Laban or Labanotation (so called after its inventor, Rudolf Laban)[2]. Another system—how accurate it is I am unable to judge from my present information—is used by the Royal Ballet[3]. Upon an admittedly superficial examination it appears to be based on much the same principles as an older system by Arthur Saint-Léon, referred to on page 8 of the present book[4].

In the 17th and 18th centuries, when dancing was simpler, there was an eminently practical system in use, the principles of which are similar to those on which Laban's is based. This was the *chorégraphie* of Pierre Beauchamps and Raoul Auger Feüillet, published in English in a translation by John Weaver in 1706 (Fig. 1A)[5]. There was, in those days, even a system of recording the steps of horses in the art of *dressage*[6].

Stepanov's system, which is described in this book, is certainly practical. One has only to read the official testomonial, signed by such people as Petipa and Johannsen to realise that. In *Theatre Street*[7], Tamara Karsavina describes how lessons in the system were given at the Imperial Ballet Schools in Russia.

Stepanov's book is no more than a skeleton key, showing but the general principles and their application[8]. One can see many possible refinements—for instance, the use of sharps and flats to modify the tension of movements—yet even as it stands, it could be used as an aid to decipher old notations (it was by means of records made in Stepanov's system that the late Nicolai Sergayev was able to revive *The Sleeping Princess* and other great Imperial ballets for Diaghilev and for more recent companies). What is even more important, it could offer ideas for the enrichment of other existing systems.

It may be, too, that Stepanov was making the first probings into a theory of spatial harmony, such as has since been embodied by Laban in the icosahedron scales.

Stepanov's notation shows a different approach from Laban's. As such it is well worthy of consideration. Great minds do not necessarily think alike, and at least in the present instance one may well have something of value to offer the other[9].

R.L.

BIBLIOGRAPHICAL NOTE

The original edition of Stepanov's book is of considerable rarity. A bibliographical description of the copy on which this translation is based is therefore given here. It is described by James Claydon, and is in the possession of the translator.
ALPHABET/DES/MOUVEMENTS DU CORPS HUMAIN/ (rule)/Essai d'enregistrement des mouvements/du corps humain au moyen des / signes musicaux. / Par / W. J. STÉPANOW / Artiste des Théatres Impériaux de Saint Pétersbourg / PARIS / Imprimerie M. Zouckermann Paris, 98, rue St-Antoine, 98. / 1892
Collation: i (title-page) + i (dedication) + iii (contents) + viii (introduction) + 66 (text) + i (blank) = xiii + 66 + i (blank).
Size of pages: 23cm × 14cm
The present copy is bound in leather and has mounted on the front cover a panel from the original paper wrapper:
Chorégraphie (in frame)/ALPHABET/DES MOUVEMENTS DU CORPS HUMAIN / (rule) / Essai d'enregistrement des mouvements du corps humain au moyen des / signes musicaux. / Par / W. J. STÉPANOW / Artiste des Théatres Impériaux de Saint Pétersbourg / Librairie PAUL VIGOT / 10, Rue Monsieur-le-Prince, 10 / PARIS / Tous droits réservés / Gymnastique (in frame)

A copy of Stepanov's *Alphabet* was shown at an exhibition of books on ballet at the National Book League, London in 1957. It belongs to Madame Derra de Moroda, and by the courtesy of the exhibition's organiser, Mr. Ivor Guest, the translator was able to examine it.

It is exactly the same edition as the copy from which the present translation was made, but is still in its original paper wrapper, which shows the price of the book, printed in a cartouche on the bottom cover, thus: Prix: 3 fr. 50

The paper wrapper is glued on to the spine of the book, which is sewn in six sections, whereas the translator's copy is in five sections.

One other minor difference is that in the translator's copy, the first block of the complementary signs for circular movements (Fig. 17A in this translation) is missing. In Madame de Moroda's copy it is present.

REPORT OF THE COMMISSION OF THE IMPERIAL BALLET COMPANY OF SAINT PETERSBURG

The chair was taken by the Manager of the Imperial Ballet Company, Councillor of State J. J. Rioumine, and the following members were present: The *Maîtres de Ballet* of the Imperial Theatres M. J. Petipa and L. I. Ivanov. Artists of the same Theatres E. O. Wazem, Ch. P. Johannsen and P. A. Gerdt. The Commission had for secretary the *Régisseur* of the Imperial Theatres, W. J. Langhammer.

The Commission of the Imperial Ballet Company of Saint Petersburg has examined, 24th February 1891, a new system of movement notation, invented by Artist of the Imperial Theatres, Vladimir Ivanovitch Stepanov, to be put in practice in choreographic art. Mr. Stepanov's system had been first examined by a special commission and tested in practice in the classes of the Theatre School at Saint Petersburg. Indeed the members of this Commission and the artists have studied the system of notation of bodily movements invented by Mr. Stepanov, and they have found it all practical and applicable for the notation of ballets.

The Commission of the Imperial Ballet Company, after having studied the invention of Artist V. I. Stepanov and having tested in practice the system he has shown us, of writing down ballets by means of musical signs, have concluded unanimously that this invention constitutes an absolutely new method for rendering in an exact and regular way the movements of the body as applied to choreographic art.

Considering that up to the present no convenient means or system for the notation of ballets has existed, the Commission is of the opinion that the new system discovered by Mr. V. I. Stepanov fills this gap and will render valuable services to the art of choreography. The members of the Commission certify this by the present written report.

J. Rioumine, M. Petipa, L. Ivanov, P. A. Gerdt, Ch. P. Johannsen, E. Wazem.

Countersigned by the Secretary: W. Langhammer
True Copy.
Business Manager: Krachevsky

INTRODUCTION

It is undeniable that ordinary language is inadequate to express or to describe our own movements, or those we see being made around us. The common expressions used to convey the appearance of movement are usually too vague, too metaphorical to define any given movement or to state its dimensions accurately. It is no exaggeration to say that movements are almost as difficult as musical sounds to express in words. One has only to think of the complexity of nearly all movements of the human body to realise the truth of that. In particular, physiologists, in describing the motive functions of the various parts of the body, are well aware of the regrettable deficiency of language. To overcome the difficulties caused by the absence of adequate verbal expressions, science uses a graphic method by means of which the appearance of movement may be recorded in a recognisable manner. It shows the vital part of the body actually in movement, for example the heart, which records its movements by means of an ingenious apparatus, the *cardiograph*[10]; the outlines given by this apparatus are, so to speak, the language of the body in motion; it traces clearly and precisely all details of movements, the order in which they are made, their force, their duration, their relations with arterial pulsation and so on.

A great many other similar apparatuses are used by doctors and physiologists for the study of all sorts of physiological and pathological movements. Thus, for studying in detail the movements of the foot in walking and running, there is an apparatus constructed on the same principles as the cardiograph: the *hodograph*. This apparatus is used with specially prepared shoes, and records all details of foot movements. In making the subject cover a certain given distance with different paces one obtains by the hodograph signs which express all that is relative to the foot both in motion and at rest, likewise the movements' phases.

It is certain that this method of recording is almost mathematically exact, but unhappily its application is limited, and it is likely for a long time to remain purely a laboratory process for recording certain peculiarities of movement. The recording apparatus, at any rate in its present form, could never be the basis of a true language expressing the varied and complex play of the muscles of the human body. The outlines which it gives remain incomprehensible in the majority of cases.

The greatest experts themselves are perplexed when required, for example, to describe the complex movements of an invalid. Here for instance is a description of choreic movements[11], made by M. Charcot, the eminent director of *La Salpêtrière*[12]: "The arms simulate the movements of a tambour player, the girl stamps on the floor at regular intervals, as if beating time; at the same time the head turns rapidly from right to left." (*Charcot. Leçons du Mardi.* p.150).

This description, full of metaphor, well shows the imperfections of language for writing down movements of the human body. In such a case the recording apparatuses do not say much. They can state only certain regularities, a certain rhythm and that is all. In other cases " the graphic representations supply no precise formula; the outlines are absolutely irregular and illogical, so far as I can see."[13]. M. Charcot adds that " for describing movements of that nature one would need to be a *maître de ballet* at the *Opéra.*"

We profoundly disagree with the illustrious teacher. A *maître de ballet* would be able easily to copy the movements of a choreic subject, but he would be unable to do more than M. Charcot himself to describe them, due to the lack of a special language indispensable to such description.

In the art of the dance proper, the need of a system of dance notation has been felt for centuries. The first attempts at notation were made in the 16th century by Canon Jean Taboureau (*Thoinet Arbeau*)[14] and notwithstanding the work and subsequent refinements of such masters of the art as Beauchamp (Fig. 1A), Favier, Desais, Feüillet, Duport, Saint-Léon and others, these attempts have not been at all successful.

The latest work to deal with this question [15, 15A] was by Mr. Zorn. His system, which is a not very happy modification of Saint-Léon's, is a schematic figuration of the movements of the human body. An example, taken from Mr. Zorn's *Atlas* is shown in Fig. 1. It clearly shows the primitive method employed by the author.

It need not surprise us that in the absence of a reliable method of recording dances the progress of choreographic art has been checked; ballet, the highest dance form, has not followed the progressive path of other arts in spite of the genius of many illustrious *maîtres de ballet*. It may be assumed that some of the finest manifestations of choreographic genius have been lost for ever, because, being transmitted by memory from generation to generation, in time they pass away completely without a trace for posterity. In France, for example, who can say what has been lost of the works of *maîtres de ballet* and artists, which are now no more than a vague idea? Lastly, the composition of a new ballet presents numerous difficulties for its creator, for he is deprived of any means of noting and sketching dances preliminary to the staging of his work; he is thus deprived of the means of preparation enjoyed by the practitioner of other arts.

Moreover, the absence of a regulated method of recording movements prevents the artist from creating a choreographic theory indispensable to the development of the art of ballet; a theory that would permit the classification of an infinite number of bodily movements, which would establish the standards of a harmony of movements.

The new method of the notation of movement by musical signs which I wish to show in this book is an attempt to create a kind of alphabet for choreographers and all others who require to record human movements. The basis of the system is the analysis of all the movements of the human body in simple elementary movements, and the notation of these movements by means of musical signs and a number of supplementary signs. The combination of these notes and signs forms the alphabet, by means of which any position and any movement of the body may be recorded exactly.

We have purposely chosen musical notes because many people associate the language of movement with that of sound.

Musical notes moreover express not only the determination of sounds and their combinations but also their duration and character. In the notes of movements we try to express the same things.

The first chapters of our book deal with the recording of elementary movements of legs, arms, of torso and head; in the chapters following we shall describe the movements and their notation by our system. Finally the reader will find in our book examples of notation of classical dance steps and gymnastic exercises. These are given to accentuate the system's many advantages and to show to those engaged in gymnastic education how pupils may be shown the *angle, duration, rhythm* of any given movement—qualities which are so clearly expressed that no further explanation is needed from the teacher or composer.

Our system has been applied in practice[16], in particular for the notation of dances and whole ballets, at trials such as those made at Saint Petersburg under the control of a special commission of the *corps de ballet*. The results are given in a report drawn up by the said commission, to which, in order to avoid repetition, I refer the reader. (See page 5).

This book shows the general basis of my system by which dances and ballets may be written down. The details of the alphabet of movements and its practical application are the subject of future publications.

I hope that the general basis of the alphabet of movements which I have shown will be favourably received both amongst artists and all others who need to record the complexities of movements of the human body.

I thank in advance all those who may wish to send me their suggestions and observations.

Paris. December 1891.

ANATOMICAL NOTES

Before expounding the system of movement notation I think it will be useful to glance rapidly over the subject of human anatomy, which has guided me in the composition of my system.

The practical application of the system will be easily understood without detailed anatomical data; it will not delay the reader for long.

The human skeleton (Figs. 2 & 3) is conceived in the form of a system of levers. This system supports the muscles which, under nervous impulse, are contracted and move the levers. All bodily movements depend upon the contraction of muscles on the bones of the skeleton.

Although the muscles are considered to be the basis of all phenomena of movement, the elasticity of the bones and the ligaments also play an important part in these movements.

The physiologist who studies the mechanism of human movement takes the anatomical basis of the whole motive apparatus for the mainspring of his researches; that is to say the exact descriptions of the muscles, nerves, bones, articulations and so on. But for our purpose the most important part is the mechanism of the human skeleton.

The skeleton may be divided into three main parts: the skull, the trunk and the limbs.

The spinal column forms the foundation of the trunk. It supports the head at the top and fits solidly on the pelvis at its base. The spinal column is at once a flexible and solid support, consisting of twenty-four superimposed pieces, each pierced with a central tube. It is not straight, but convex in front in the vertical plane, concave at the back, and in addition convex in the lumbar region; it thus describes three undulating curves.

Except for the two first, the vertebrae are of a common shape. Each is formed of the three following parts: 1 body, 2 bow, 3 apophyses situated on the former. The bows of the vertebrae are joined to form a tube which contains the spinal marrow (Fig. 4). The vertebrae are joined by cartilages of different sizes which give elasticity to the spinal column.

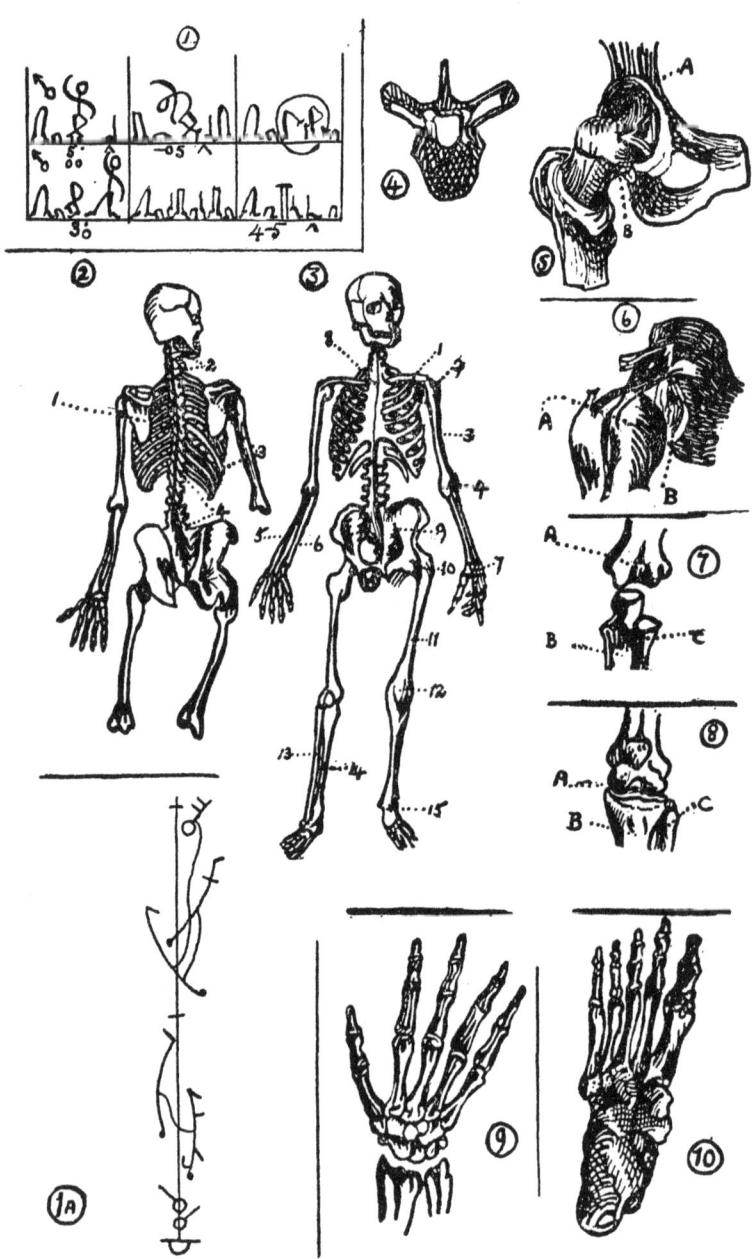

The thoracic cage is formed in front by the breast-bone, at the back by the dorsal vertebrae and laterally by the ribs, which are joined to the breast-bone by means of intercostal cartilages; so that, during respiration, the thoracic cage may be considerably dilated.

The upper limbs are attached to the trunk by the shoulders, the lower limbs by the pelvis.

The shoulder is formed by the shoulder-blade and the collar-bone. The shoulder-blade, through its articulation, is a continuation of the arm, which is formed at the top by the humerus, lower down by the two bones of the forearm; these are the radius and the ulna, the first corresponding to the thumb, the second to the little finger. Finally we have the hand, with a characteristic structure, containing as it does the eight small bones of the wrist, the five bones of the metacarpus, and phalanxes (Fig. 9).

The lower limb is composed thus: in the first place we have the femur, then the lower leg, composed of a fibula and tibia; these parts are continued to the foot with its seven tarsus bones, its five metatarsus bones and its phalanxes (Fig. 10).

To sum up, the skeleton consists of a great number of bones which are joined and articulated in diverse ways. None of them is completely static, but some have so little movement that we need not consider them.

Articulations are possible where two or more bones have their smooth gristle-covered surfaces touching and are reinforced by ligaments. The degree of mobility of an articulated joint depends upon the form of the articular surfaces and upon the disposition of the ligaments, which assist some movements and limit others. Anatomists, in consideration of this, recognise several categories of mobility. For our purpose, however, it is sufficient to say that certain forms of articulation permit movement in every direction, others in two opposed directions; finally there are those not included in the other two categories.

To the first kind of articulation belong those of the shoulder (scapulo-humeral, Fig. 5) and of the pelvis (coxo-femoral, Fig. 6). These are arranged so that a spherical surface on one bone fits into a spherical cavity in the other. In this case the first bone may be moved in every direction, but the extent of the movement depends on the form of the cavity; the shallower this is, the more unrestricted the movement; contrariwise the deeper it is, the more limited will be the movement. The articulation of the shoulder may serve as an example in the first case, that of the thigh in the second case. That is why the movements of the arms are more unrestricted than those of the legs.

In coxo-femoral articulations the movements are made around three principal axes, contained in an angle of 90°. The broader movements of this articulation are flexion and extension (that is to say the lowering and raising of the pelvis). In these states the bones of the articulation form an angle. The maximum angle of flexion of a leg is 76°; that of extension does not exceed 10°; if the knee is bent the flexion may be as much as 115°.

The other forms of movement in this articulation are adduction and abduction. In abduction the thigh is withdrawn outward from the median line, in adduction it is brought closer. Further movements made by this articulation are those of rotation and circumgyration. In the first the extremity of the bone describes an arc around its own axis; in circumgyration it describes a conic surface around an axis.

The articulation of the shoulder governs a larger group of articulations than any other part of the body. Not only are its own movements more varied on the actual articulary surfaces, but the whole shoulder describes a series of movements which help other articulations in their movements[17].

The flexion and extension of the articulation (or the raising and lowering of the arms) are limited. The maximum flexion is 63° or 64°, and the extension 20° or 21°.

The largest movements in this articulation are abduction and adduction. Abduction consists of raising the arms outwards. In adduction the arms are carried beyond the horizontal position, the whole shoulder being involved. In this articulation rotation is freely made up to 90°.

Elbow and knee articulations (Figs. 7 & 8) belong to the class that permits the principal movements in one direction, which in this case is diametral. These movements are the flexion and extension of the forearm and of the leg.

In the articulation of the knee we again have rotary movement, but for this the knee must at the same time be bent. The more the knee is bent the broader is the rotation and when the knee forms an angle of 90°, it attains its maximum. The outside rotation approaches 30°, inside 10°.

The rotation of the forearm is not made in the articulation of the elbow, but in the cubito-radial articulation.

The articulations of the foot and wrist are complicated in form. In the first, the principal bone is the ankle-bone which moves upward with the shin-bone and the fibula, downward with the heel-bone, and forward with the scaphoid. The series of articulations of the wrist are found between the lower part of the bones of the forearm, on one side, and of the bones of the metacarpus on the other.

In both cases we may discern movements in two directions. The movements around the horizontal axis are flexion and extension, the movements around the perpendicular axis, abduction and adduction.

Just a few words about a category of articulations in which the bones of articulation provide the axis around which another makes its movement. Such is the classic example of the first two vertebrae. The second vertebra (axis) presents to the front an apophysis (odontoid) which forms an axis on which the movement of the first vertebra (axis) with the skull is made.

In the sideways movements of the head, the atlas moves around the odontoid apophysis and describes a somewhat extended arc. Another example in this category is the cubito-radial articulation.

CHAPTER I
NOTES AND SIGNS

These glimpses into the subject of anatomy as applicable to movement, although brief, are nevertheless sufficient to make comprehensible the basis of the system which the author now has the honour to present to the public.

Our method is based on the same principles as musical notation.

Primarily, we take as our principle that human movements belong to two categories, principal and secondary[18]. Principal movements are those of the whole torso and of whole limbs. They are made in the following directions: forward (flexion), sideways (abduction), and backward (extension). These principal movements are written down by our system as follows.

There are two forms of notes that are placed in the stave (Fig. 11) to indicate the movements: the oblong form to indicate contact with the ground (Fig. 19), the round form for indicating jumping or gestures in the air, that is, without contact with the ground (Fig. 20). There are two other forms, one for the right leg and arm (Fig. 12A), the other for the left leg and arm (Fig. 12B).

It may be seen already that these notes placed in various ways can indicate various movements, but the possibilities of the method will be better understood if we add that each stave has its clef governing the part of the body to which the stave belongs, giving the normal position, and thus the principal movements of each part[19]. In Fig. 11, A is the stave for the torso and the head (simultaneously); B for the arms; C for the legs. In Fig. 24, A is the note of the normal position; B, forward; C, backward; D, to the right; E, to the left.

The notes indicate, it is true, the first degree of the movements, but to obtain its second, third and succeeding degrees we have only to take advantage, as in music, of supplementary lines. We will examine these indicators in the following chapters.

In taking the angle of 45° for the first degree of movement a scale is obtained of absolute principal movements indentical to a musical scale. Figure 25 is the scale of movements of the torso; Figure 26 of the arms; Figure 29 of the legs.

We then indicate secondary movements by the complementary signs shown as follows.

Fig. 13. Complementary sign for flexion of symmetrical parts or forward movement of symmetrical parts.

Fig. 14. Complementary sign for extension of symmetrical parts or backward movement of symmetrical parts.

Fig. 15. Complementary sign for adduction of symmetrical parts or movement to the right of symmetrical parts.

Fig. 16. Complementary sign for abduction of symmetrical parts or movement to the left of symmetrical parts.

Fig. 17. Complementary signs for rotation.

Fig. 17A. Complementary signs for circular movements.

Fig. 18A. Complementary sign for enlargement of a movement.

Fig. 18B. Complementary sign for dimunition of a movement.

These are all the notes and signs of which our system consists. Experience has shown that it is possible by their means, to write down all movements of the human body—either together or in part.

CHAPTER II
LEG MOVEMENTS
Principal Movements

The signs employed in our system to write down the principal leg movements are shown in Fig. 21[20].

Forward movements are written as shown in Fig. 21A. For the left leg by a note on the third line; for the right leg by a note on the second line.

Sideways movements are written as shown in Fig. 21B. For the left leg, movement to the left, by a note between the third and fourth lines; for the right leg, movement to the right, by a note between the second and third lines.

Backward movements are written as shown in Fig. 21C. For the left leg, by a note on the fourth line, and for the right leg by a note on the first line.

To sum up, if we wish to obtain the written reproduction of the principal movements, we place the leg clef on the stave, and we have the notes shown in Fig. 27.

It will be seen that the notes determine the direction of the leg movements very distinctly. However, it is also necessary to determine the exact dimension of the movements and to express them by our system. In the first place the anatomical measurements of the maximum angles of the principal movements are given as follows: movement of elevation, forward, 76°; the same movement sideways, 45°; finally backward, 10°[21].

The angles may be enlarged if the movement is accompanied by the inclination of the pelvis in the condition which results from one foot being on the ground while the other is raised.

Figs. 31 and 32 give the idea of these movements and show the degrees that may be recorded in our system[22]. The position of the legs CD and CD1, Fig. 31, determine the first degree of sideways raising: the angles BCD and BCD1 each equal 45°. The position of the legs CE and CE1 determines the second degree, the angles BCE and BCE1 each being equal to 90°.

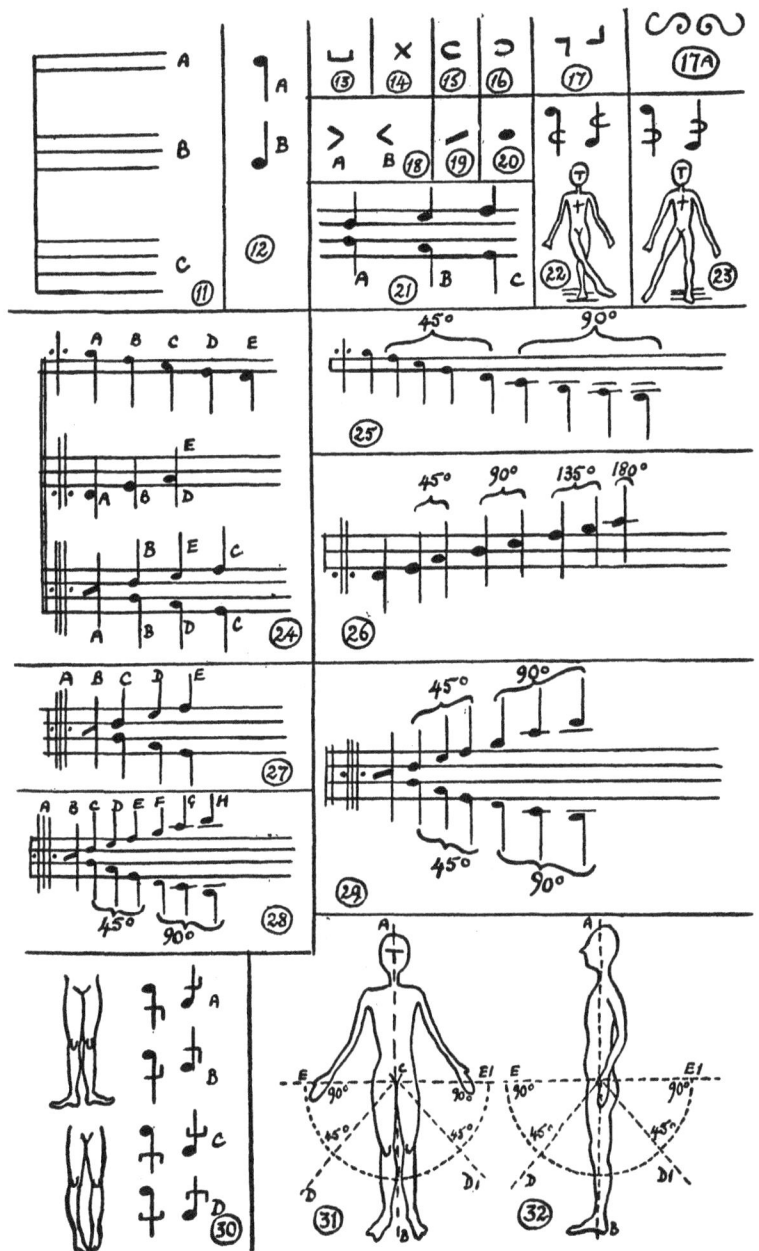

Fig. 32 shows movements of the legs in front and behind; we have here the same degrees of elevation as in the preceding figure.

After having thus classified the movements according to their degrees, it is easy for us to express them in our stave by having recourse to complementary lines. We thus obtain our scale of principal movements for each limb (Fig. 28).

Secondary Movements

The coxo-femoral articulation carries all the principal leg movements. The same articulation also gives the following secondary movements: 1 Movements of adduction and abduction of the raised leg. 2 Rotary movements. Fig. 22 shows the movement of adduction of the raised leg. Fig. 23 shows the abduction of the raised leg.

The movements of which we speak are shown in our system by complementary signs placed on the tail of the note. These signs are also shown in Figs. 22 and 23. They indicate equally that the angle of abduction or adduction will be 45°.

According to man's anatomical construction, each foot is turned out in the region of 30°; this deviation forms what may be called the normal rotation (see Fig. 31).

Rotation of the leg is made in two directions only: outwards and inwards. Rotation outwards (Fig. 30, top) is marked by signs placed on the tail of the note as shown in Fig. 30A. Rotation inwards (Fig. 30, bottom) is marked by variations of the same sign as shown in Fig. 30B. These signs indicate also that the measure of the angle of rotation is 30° from the normal position.

Choreographic art particularly recognises a rotation of 45° as part of the normal position. Figs. 30C and 30D show how we write down this rotation, which we call the second degree of rotation—Fig. 30C: rotation outwards, Fig. 30D: rotation inwards.

Knee Movements

All movements consequent on the articulation of the knee are reduced to three degrees of bending. Fig. 33 shows those movements that are expressed in our system by complementary signs placed on the tail of the note. The leg ACB placed on

ACD forms the first degree of bending, giving an angle BCD, of 45°. We express this for the two legs as shown in Fig. 34A. Arriving at the position ACE, the leg gives an angle BCE, which equals 90°. This is the second degree of bending which we write by the signs in Fig. 34B. Finally, the leg placed in the position ACF forms the angle BCF of 135°, the third degree of bending, which our system writes as in Fig. 34C.

Foot Movements

Movements of the foot are bending (plantar flexion), extension (dorsal flexion), adduction, abduction and rotation.

Anatomical measurements of these movements give the following angles: flexion, 40°; extension, 27°; adduction, 16°; abduction, 6°; rotation inwards, 10°; rotation outwards, 20°. The following are the complementary signs, placed in these cases before the note, which are used in our system for the notation of these movements.

Fig. 35 shows flexion and extension. The foot AB, having arrived at the position AD, forms an angle of 40°. This position is written by the sign shown in Fig. 36A. The practice of choreography makes it possible to enlarge this angle to 60°— in some cases as much as 70°—and we note this position as the second degree of flexion and show it by the sign in Fig. 36B. The foot AB in the position AC shows the inverse movement (extension). This position is shown in Fig. 36C.

Fig. 37A shows the normal position of the foot, Fig. 37B its adduction and its sign, Fig. 37C its abduction and sign.

Fig. 38A shows the outward rotation of the foot and its sign, Fig. 38B its inward rotation and sign.

Contact of the Foot with the Ground

The contact of the foot with the ground may be complete or partial. Complete contact of the foot with the ground is shown by an oblong note, as has already been described (Page 16). Partial contact, that is to say when the toes alone touch the ground (Fig. 39), is shown by a vertical line beside the line of the foot (Fig. 39A). Choreographic art has another position— contact with the ground by the point of the foot only (*sur les pointes*). We note this position by three vertical lines (Fig. 39B). Finally contact with the ground by the heel alone is shown as in Fig. 39C.

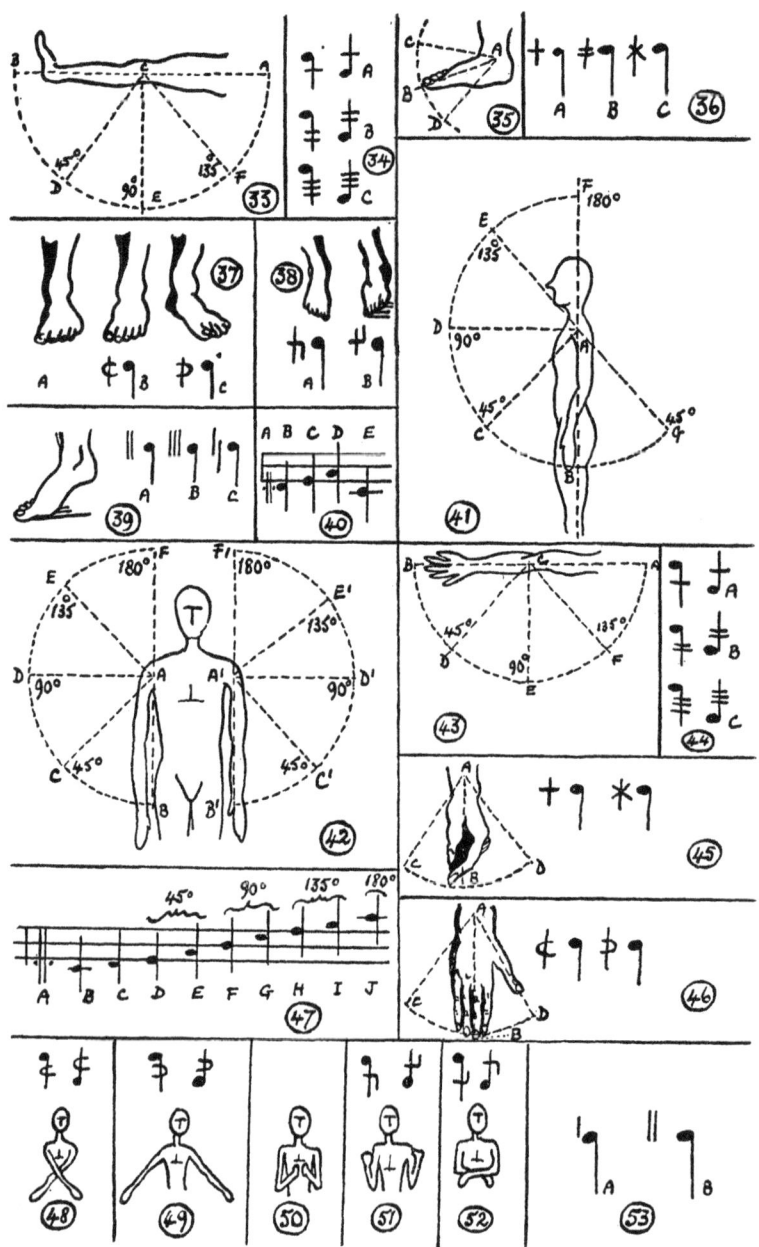

CHAPTER III
ARM MOVEMENTS
Principal Movements

The principal movements of the articulation of the shoulder may be reduced to the raising of the arms in front (flexion), at the side (abduction) and backward (extension).

For writing down these movements in our system, the same rules are followed as for leg movements; that is to say that the bottom tail indicates the right arm and the upper tail the left arm. Fig. 40 shows: A, clef of arm movements; B, note of normal position; C, note of movement of arms forward; D, sideways; E, backward.

Figs. 41 and 42 show the degrees of the movements envisaged in our system. We thus divide the movements of elevation of the arms into four degrees. The first degree gives an angle of 45°, the second one of 90°, the third one of 135°, the fourth one of 180°.

The elevation of the arms in the scapulo-humeral articulation may be said to be lifted through the following angles: 64° forward; 65° sideways; 21° backward. If the elevation is continued as far as 90°, 135° and 180° (see Figs. 41 and 42), the movement of the humerus involves that of the shoulder blade.

In indicating the degrees of elevation by notes we have the *scale of principal arm movements*, shown in Fig. 47. A, clef of arm movements; B, raising of arms backward; C, note of normal position; D, raising of arms forward; E, sideways; F, forward; G, sideways; H, forward; I, sideways; J, upward (maximum elevation).

Secondary Movements

Secondary movements of the arms resulting from the articulation of the shoulder are adduction and abduction of the raised arms, and rotation. Fig. 48 shows the adduction, Fig. 49 the abduction of the raised arms, and the notes by which they are written in our system. The signs also show the angle of movement to be 45°.

Rotation of the arms is possible in two different directions: outwards and inwards[23]. Fig. 50 shows the normal position of the arms, elbows bent. Fig. 51 shows the degree of rotation outwards, Fig. 52 the degree of rotation inwards, and the notes by which these movements are written.

Movements of the Elbow

The movement of the elbow, like that of the knee, is reduced to three degrees of flexion, indicated by signs placed on the tail of the note.

Fig. 43 shows these movements. Position CD of the forearm forms the first degree of flexion; angle BCD equals 45°. This movement is shown by the signs illustrated in Fig. 44A. Position CE represents the second degree. The angle of this position is 90° and is shown by the signs in Fig. 44B. The third degree is the position CF, an angle of 135°, written as in Fig. 44C.

Movements of the Wrist

Wrist movements comprise flexion, extension, adduction, abduction and rotation. According to anatomical measurements, these different movements give angles of 84° for flexion, 68° for extension, 27° for adduction and 35° for abduction.

Our system indicates these movements by complementary signs on the line preceding the note. Fig. 45 shows the flexion and extension of the wrist. The wrist AB, arriving at the position AC forms an angle of 45°, written by the left hand sign in Fig. 45. In the position AD the wrist gives an extension of 45°, shown by the right hand sign in the same figure.

Fig. 46 shows the abduction (AC) and adduction (AD) of the wrist (AB). The sign of adduction is that shown at the left side in the same figure; that of abduction is on the right side.

Fig. 54A shows the outward rotation of the wrist (written as in Fig. 55A), Fig. 54B the inward rotation (written as in Fig. 55B).

There are also signs for finger movements. Half-flexion of the fingers is noted by a vertical line (Fig. 53A) placed beside the line on which the wrist movements are shown, complete flexion by two lines similarly placed (Fig. 53B).

Shoulder Movements

Each shoulder is capable of moving in the following directions: forward, backward and upward. For showing these different movements we use notes complementary to the principal notes of each arm.

Fig. 56A shows the shoulder's movement forward, written as shown in the following figures; Fig. 57A for the right shoulder, Fig. 57B for the left shoulder, and Fig. 57C for two shoulders.

Fig. 56B shows the shoulder's movement backward. This is written as shown in Fig. 57D (right shoulder), Fig. 57E (left shoulder), Fig. 57F (two shoulders).

Fig. 56C shows the shoulders' movement upward. This is written as shown in Fig. 57G (right shoulder), Fig. 57H (left shoulder), Fig. 57I (two shoulders).

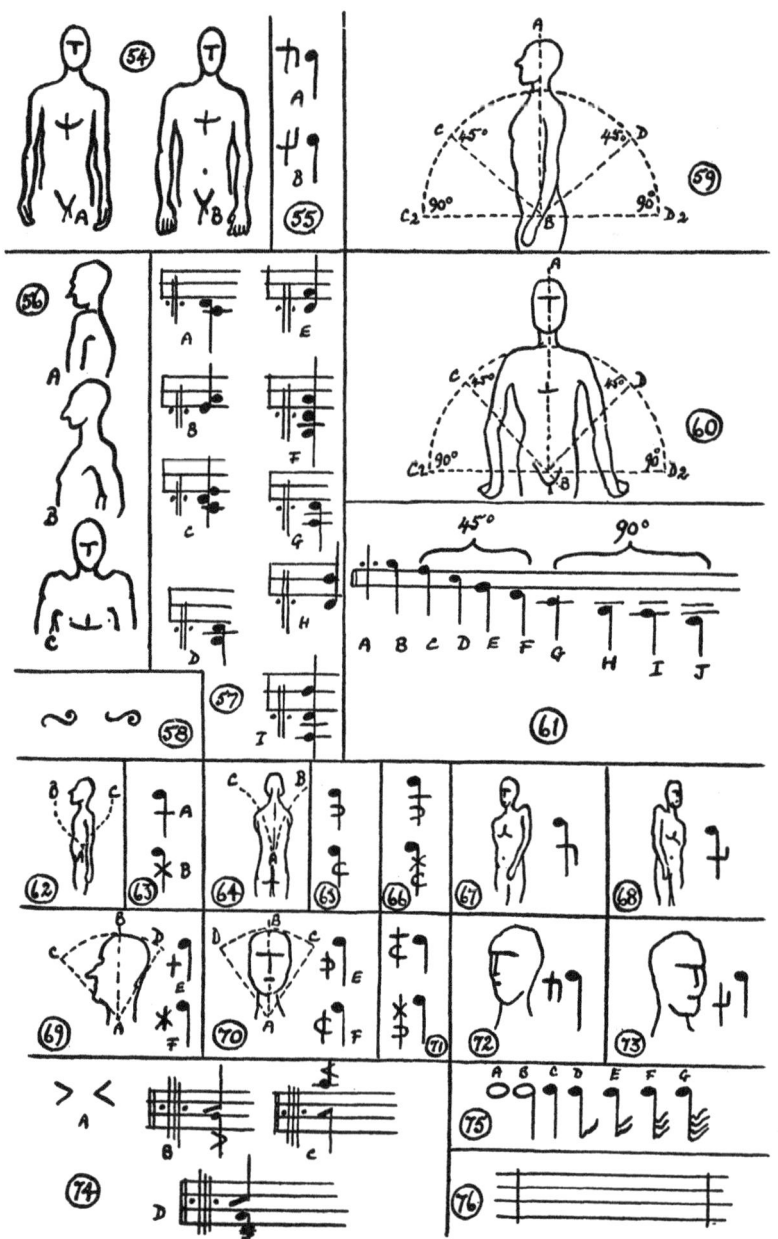

CHAPTER IV
MOVEMENTS OF THE TORSO
Principal Movements

The principal movements of the torso are: forward, backward, to the right, to the left. Figs. 59 and 60 show their degrees. The torso in position CB (Fig. 59) is in the first degree of the forward movement: angle ABC equals 45°; position C₂B forms the second degree, the angle of which is 90°. In position BD (Fig. 59) the torso is at the first degree of backward movement; angle ABD equals 45°; position BD₂ shows the second degree, the angle of which equals 90°.

In Fig. 60 we show the movements of the torso to right and left, in which may be found the same angles of 45°, 90° etc.

The movements are thus graduated according to their angles, which are easily expressed in our system with the help of supplementary lines. Fig. 61 shows: A, clef of torso movements; B, note of normal position; C, note of forward movement of torso; D, to the right; E, backward; F, to the left; G, forward; H, to the right; I, backward; J, to the left.

Secondary Movements

Secondary movements of the torso may be reduced to the flexion of the spinal column simultaneously with the shoulders. In our system these movements are shown by complementary signs placed on the tail of the note of the torso.

Fig. 62 shows the movements of the spinal column forward (written as in Fig. 63A) and backward (written as in Fig. 63B). Fig. 64 represents the movements of the spinal column to the right and left (written as in Fig. 65 top and bottom).

These movements are possible in more directions than those just stated: forward and to the right, forward and to the left, backward and to the right, backward and to the left. Movements such as these are shown by two signs, indicating a simultaneous movement. Two examples are shown in Fig. 66.

Fig. 67 represents the rotation of the spinal column to the right, Fig. 68 the same rotation to the left. Each is written as shown in the same figures.

Head Movements

Head movements may be reduced to inclinations in all directions, and rotation. These again are shown by complementary signs placed on the line which precedes the torso note. Fig. 69 shows the inclination of the head forward (written as in Fig. 69E), and backward (written as Fig. 69F). Fig. 70 shows inclination of the head to right (written as Fig. 70E), and to left (written as Fig. 70F). The angle of each inclination equals 45°.

Between these two principal directions there are intermediate movements which the head may make. Such movements are noted, as in analagous movements of the spinal column, by two signs indicating the two directions, in the intervals of which the movements are made. Examples are shown in Fig. 71.

Rotary movements of the head are made in two directions: to right and to left. Fig. 72 shows rotation to the right (written as shown in the same figure), Fig. 73 rotation to the left (written as shown in the same figure). The angle of movement equals 45° in both cases.

Circular Movements

We are aware of circular movements, or movements of circumgyration, which are made when the extremity of a bone describes a conic surface around an apparent axis. Among such movements may be placed those of the wrist. Such movements may be written in our system by the method used for secondary movements, and using the signs shown in Fig. 58.

Signs of Increase and Decrease

Each movement may be enlarged or diminished to the correct degree by use of the signs shown in Fig. 74A. The examples shown in Figs. 74B, C and D demonstrate the practical application of these signs. In the first example the forward movement of the right leg is enlarged, that is to say the angle of movement equals 45° plus 22½°. The second example gives the dimunition of the movement to the second degree; the angle of the movement equals 90° less 22½°. The third example shows the dimunition of the movement to the second degree in the articulation of the knee; the angle of movement equals 90° less 22½°.

It is thus that our system may be used to write down the increase and decrease of all other movements.

CHAPTER V
DURATION AND ARRANGEMENT OF THE NOTES

Not only does a note determine the character of its movement, it also indicates its duration. The same signs are used as in music for this. All are illustrated in Fig. 75. Their names are: A, semibreve; B, minim; C, crotchet; D, quaver; E, semiquaver; F, demisemiquaver; G, semidemisemiquaver.

The value of these notes is exactly the same as in music. One semibreve equals two minims; one minim, two crotchets; one crotchet, two quavers; one quaver, two semiquavers; one semiquaver, two demisemiquavers; one demisemiquaver, two semidemisemiquavers.

Generally we adopt musical expressions for regulating the general pace of the movements. Thus, *adagio*, sedate and broad, indicates that the semibreve is of tolerably long duration, and on this duration depends the value of the other notes. Here are the various expressions used.

Italian	*English*
Largo	Broad and slow
Lento	Slow
Adagio	Sedate and broad
Andante	Moderately slow
Moderato	Moderate
Allegro	Quick
Vivace	Brisk, lively
Presto	Fast

These are relative expressions. In order to obtain a rigorously exact timing the use of a metronome is necessary[24].

The general times, largo, lento and so on, are subdivided into equal intervals called bars which are shown by perpendicular lines placed on the stave (Fig. 76).

The bars are divided into two categories: measures of two (or four) or of three beats to the bar. At the commencement of the first bar is placed a fraction in which the numerator

indicates the category of the measure, and the denominator the number of its parts. (See Figs. 77, *duple*, and 78, *triple*).

A point, or dot, placed after a note, indicates that the note which precedes it is augmented to half its value. Thus a pointed minim equals three crotchets (Fig. 79, top), a pointed crotchet equals three quavers (Fig. 79, bottom) and so on.

It is useful to state separately the duration of the notes for each leg, likewise for each arm. Fig. 80 shows, for example, how the series of movements for each leg is written on the stave. This example clearly shows us that, for each leg, the notes, while maintaining the value of the measure, that is to say 2/4, are differently and independently expressed. Fig. 81 shows the same thing applied to the arms.

When two or more notes are placed on different lines and connected by a curved line, a flowing, gliding or light movement is indicated (Fig. 82). A curve joining two notes on the same line of the stave, indicates a continuous movement (Fig. 83).

For the leg movements we have a dotted curve which indicates the displacement of the body (Fig. 84). It will be seen that in this example the left leg has made a step forward.

Finally, we add that each peculiarity of the position of the body or the part that executes a series of movements, is indicated on the clef. In the classical dances, for example, where the leg stays always in the second degree of rotation, the sign of rotation is placed on the leg clef.

CHAPTER VI
TURNS OF THE BODY

For writing incomplete turns of the body we use a system of numbers placed above the leg stave (Fig. 85, at right). Thus Number 1 corresponds to the position of the body represented by Fig. 85A. Number 2 corresponds to the turn represented by Fig. 85B; number 3 to the position shown in Fig. 85C, number 4 to that in Fig. 85D. Numbers 5, 6, 7, 8 indicate intermediate points between the four preceding ones, and subdivide the circumference into eight parts.

If we wish to determine such points with greater precision we are able, in using this system of numbers, to subdivide the circumference into sixteen, thirty-two parts and so on. We proceed in the following manner: we divide the interval between 1 and 5, and indicate the point obtained by the number 9; then we divide the interval between 5 and 2, and indicate the point obtained by the number 10, and so on.

Complete turns (called *pirouettes* in choreography) are written by means of this system of numbers, and by the following method. One first places the number which indicates the position of the body in which the movement commences, then at the side of it is placed, in brackets, another number which determines the side towards which the movement is made.

When it is desired to reproduce two or more complete turns a little number is put at the side of the closing bracket to indicate how many are to be made. For example: $1(5)^2$.

In all these cases, in uninterrupted partial turns as well as whole turns, the numbers indicating the corresponding positions are joined by a dotted line, as in Fig. 86.

CHAPTER VII
GYMNASTICS

Here are a number of gymnastic exercises, the movements of which we have reproduced by means of our system. The exercises are taken from " Manuel d'Exercises Gymnastiques du Ministère de l'Instruction Publique et des Beaux Arts."

EXERCISE A
Simultaneous flexion and extension of upper and lower limbs.
(Figure 93)
1. Bend the left leg and thigh in bringing the hands to the shoulders.
2. Stretch forward the leg and the arms.
3. Return to position 1.
4. Stand.

Repeat the movement with the right leg.
The extension of the arm may be made horizontally, laterally or vertically.

EXERCISE B
To raise oneself on tiptoe; with arm movements.
(Figure 94)
1. Hands on shoulders, palms closed.
2. Rise on tiptoe and stretch arms and fingers vertically.
3. Bend the arms and stay on tiptoe.
4. Stand.

This movement may be executed in two parts, the arms extended with lateral elevation, elevation in front, and complete circumgyration of the arms.

EXERCISE C
Bending of legs with arms extended. (Preparation for jumping).
(Figure 95)
Position: Standing, the arms raised and extended.
1. Bend the legs; briskly lower the arms and carry them in backward abduction.

2. Straighten the legs again immediately, briskly projecting the arms in the air without bending them.

In position 1 the body is carried on tiptoe, the knees slightly strained.

EXERCISE D

Combined movement of the trunk, arms and legs.

(Figure 96)

1. Raise the arms vertically without bending them, the fingers extended.
2. Flexion of the body with lowering of the arms.
3. Flexion of legs with arms raised horizontally.
4. Hands on the ground.
5. Extension of legs, standing on the hands and the toes.
6 and 7. Flexion and extension of the arms, the elbow well stretched.
8. Return to the crouching position, arms in front.
9. Stand.

EXERCISE E

Hopping with flexion of the trunk.

(Figure 97)

The pupils hop in place, vigorously lifting and extending their legs in front while hopping, returning after each descent to the standing position.

CHAPTER VIII
CHOREOGRAPHY

The aim of this book is to present to the public a new method of writing down the movements of the body, of creating, so to speak, an alphabet of movements suitable for introduction into the art of the dance.

The alphabet may be useful for the doctor to note the choreic movements of an invalid, as well as for the gymnast to write down his exercises and for a dancer to study dance movements.

In general, dances are the combination of elementary bodily movements, combinations which are easy to analyse. It is easy to see how simply they may be written down by our system. In the following figures we show, by way of example, how many of the well-known forms of the classical dance are written. Incidentally, it will be seen how the characteristic position of the legs in these movements is shown on the clef (Fig. 87).

The first position is written as in Fig. 88. The fifth position with right foot forward and left foot behind as in Fig. 89; with left foot forward and right foot behind as in Fig. 90. The third position in its capacity of diminished fifth position is written as shown in Fig. 91.

Figure 92 shows the five positions. A, clef for the legs; B, first position; C, second position; D, third position, right leg in front; E, third position, left leg in front; F, fourth position, right leg in front; G, fourth position, left leg in front; H, fifth position, right leg in front; I, fifth position, left leg in front.

The remainder of the figures show the steps as tabulated below.

Fig. 98 Petits battements tendus
Fig. 99 Pas coupés
Fig. 100 Battements fondus
Fig. 101 Ronds de jambe en dehors et en dedans à terre
Fig. 102 Ronds de jambe en dehors et en dedans en l'air
Fig. 103 Grands battements
Fig. 104 Petits battements sur le cou de pied

Fig. 105 Assemblés
Fig. 106 Pas jetés
Fig. 107 Pas ballonés
Fig. 108 Pas balottés
Fig. 109 Pas glissés
Fig. 110 Changement des pieds
Fig. 111 Entrechat trois
Fig. 112 Entrechat quatre
Fig. 113 Entrechat six
Fig. 114 Brisés Télémaque battus
Fig. 115 Entrechat sept, pas de bourré, attitude alongée, cabriole et pirouette sur le cou de pied

We have been successful in writing down entire ballets in this way, as well as dances. The conferences which have been called on this subject at the conservatoire of the Imperial Theatres of Saint Petersburg have amply shown, and the artists who have taken part in them, and who have used it to write down all details of the most complicated ballets, are convinced of the immediate and practical value of my system.

KEY TO THE ANATOMICAL ILLUSTRATIONS

Figure 2 1. Shoulder blade
2. Cervical part of the vertebrae
3. Dorsal part
4. Lumbar part

Figure 3 1. Collar bone
2. Scapulo-humeral articulation
3. Humerus
4. Articulation of the elbow
5. Radius
6. Cubit or ulna
7. Wrist
8. Breast bone
9. Pelvis
10. Coxo-femoral articulation
11. Femur
12. Articulation of the knee
13. Fibula
14. Tibia
15. Articulation of the foot

Figure 4 Vertebra

Figure 5 Scapulo-humeral articulation
A. Glenoid cavity
B. Top of the humerus

Figure 6 Coxo-femoral articulation
A. Top of the femur
B. Glenoid cavity

Figure 7 Articulation of the knee
A. Lower extremity of the femur
B. Tibia
C. Fibula

Figure 8 Articulation of the elbow
A. Lower extremity of the humerus
B. Cubit
C. Radius

Figure 9 Bones of the hand and wrist

Figure 10 Bones of the foot

NOTES

Notes by Stepanov are marked with an asterisk. The remainder are the translator's.

¹ *Effort* by Rudolf Laban and F. C. Lawrence (London, 1947).

² *Labanotation* by Ann Hutchinson (New York, 1954); *Principles of Dance Movement and Notation* by Rudolf Laban (London, 1956); *Abriss der Kinetographie Laban* von Albrecht Knust. 2 vols. (Hamburg, 1956).

³ *An Introduction to Benesh Dance Notation* by Rudolf and Joan Benesh (London, 1956).

⁴ Details of Saint-Léon's notation and of several other methods are given in *La Danse Classique* by Antonine Meunier (Paris, n.d.). This book is mainly an exposition of Mme. Meunier's own system, a kind of shorthand which is a " literary " rather than a " spatial " solution to the problems of recording movements.

⁵ *Orchesography. Or, the Art of Dancing* (London, 1706).

⁶ *A General System of Horsemanship in all its Branches* by William Cavendish, Duke of Newcastle (London, 1743).

⁷ *Theatre Street*. The Reminiscences of Tamara Karsavina (London, 1930).

⁸ After Stepanov's death in 1896, his system was considerably elaborated by A. A. Gorsky. But so far as I know the present book, and the rare French edition from which it is translated, are the only printed records of the system. But see Appendices I and II.

⁹ For those who may wish to look more deeply into the subject of dance notation there is a good reading list published by the Kamin Dance Bookshop, New York. It is *Danceomania* 43. " Check List of Books on Dance Notation from the 16th to the 20th century." Compiled by Sally Kamin.

¹⁰ An instrument which records the movements of the heart by inscribing a curve on a graph.

¹¹ Movements, that is, of one afflicted by the pathological state known as chorea or St. Vitus's Dance.

¹² A mental hospital in Paris.

¹³ *op. cit.* p.249.*

¹⁴ Arbeau's book *Orchesography* [not to be confused with Feüillet's book of the same title—see Note 5 above] exists in several modern editions. Two are in English. One is a translation by Cyril W. Beaumont; the other, more recent and still in print, is translated by Mary Stewart Evans. It is an American publication. The original edition of 1588 is of excessive rarity.

¹⁵ *Grammatik der Tanzkunst* von A. Zorn (Leipzig, 1887). Verlag von Weber.*

¹⁵ᴀAn English translation, *Grammar of the Art of Dancing*, edited by A. J. Sheafe, was published at Boston, Mass. in 1905. Both editions are rare.

In view of Stepanov's next sentence, it is interesting to note that Zorn claimed in his system to have " amplified and perfected the system of Saint-Léon." In fact, purely as a shorthand system for recording classical ballet, it has some points in its favour, particularly in its " abbreviated " signs. But it makes no serious attempt to analyse movements in the sense that Stepanov has done.

¹⁶ We have not mentioned our experiments in the notation of pathological movements (in particular those of patients suffering from chorea and hysteria) made in hospitals. Our experiences in this sphere are limited.*

41

[17] In our system we consider four categories of flexion and abduction, or, to put it in clearer terms, four degrees of raising the arms in front and at the sides: the two first movements are accomplished by articulation alone, the two others involve the shoulder.*

[18] Nevertheless there are many exceptions.*

[19] In Zorn's system the clef is used to indicate the direction in which the movement is made. It consists of an arrow attached to a small circle, pointing in the appropriate direction (Fig. 1). It is obviously adapted from similar signs in Feüillet's system, where, however, they are a more integral part of the script.

[20] In our leg stave the two lower lines are for the right leg, the two upper lines are for the left leg.*

[21] The front elevation may well give an angle of 115°, but in order to achieve this, the knee must be bent.*

[22] Zorn (*op. cit.*) uses a similar division of movement by degrees. He shows similar illustrations to Stepanov's—that is a circle or arc drawn around the body or limbs—but rather more finely divided into segments than Stepanov's. In Fig. 31, for instance, he would bisect the angle BCD to form a segment of $22\frac{1}{2}°$. This he would call the "low degree"; 45° would be "half-high"; $67\frac{1}{2}°$ "three-quarters high"; 90° "high", and 135° "super-high."

[23] Rotation in the articulation of the arms is calculated with arms bent.*

[24] Stepanov does not explain the use of the metronome more fully than this. The pendulum of the machine is graduated into a scale so that its weight may be placed in position giving from 40 to 208 audible strokes to a minute. The determination of the value of a crotchet in any given piece of music is shown as in this example: M.M.80 = ♩. This example denotes that the beat of a crotchet equals the pulse of Maelzel's metronome with the weight set at 80. Maelzel was the inventor of the machine.

APPENDIX I

Note on V. I. Stepanov based on information supplied to the translator by A. R. Tomsky, Art Director of the Ballet of the Bolshoi Theatre of the U.S.S.R.

Vladimir Ivanovich Stepanov (1866–1896) finished his studies at the St. Petersburg Ballet School in 1886, and was enrolled as a dancer in the corps de ballet in the ballet troupe of the Maryinsky Theatre. As a dancer he never rose above average, but this did not prevent his becoming one of the first champions of the creation of the science of ballet. In 1889 he entered the University of St. Petersburg as an external student, and at the same time began to work absorbedly on the creation of his system of dance notation. In 1891 his work was carefully considered by a special commission of the leading performers of the St. Petersburg Ballet Troupe and acknowledged as having the highest significance. In 1892 Stepanov went to Paris, where he published his work in the French language, in co-operation with the ballet master Gansen, who had once worked in Russia and was at that time a conductor in the ballet of the Paris *Opéra*.

On Stepanov's return to Russia, his system of notation was included in the syllabus of the Ballet School. Stepanov continued to perfect his system and, at the same time, worked out the first programme of teaching dance disciplines for the St. Petersburg Ballet School, but this did not receive the support of the directors of the School. Then Stepanov presented his proposal to the Moscow Ballet School, where it met with sympathy and was put into effect. A few years later it was also introduced into the St. Petersburg School.

At the same time, the Moscow School of Ballet wished also to include in its programme a study of Stepanov's system of notation. In connexion with this, he went to Moscow in 1896 in order to acquaint the board of directors of the School with his principle and to put it into teaching practice. In Moscow, Stepanov became ill and died.

During the time when Stepanov was working on the creation of his system, a young St. Petersburg dancer, A. A. Gorsky (1871–1924), became one of his most fervent admirers and helpers. After Stepanov's death, Gorsky considered it his moral duty to continue the work of his dead colleague. In 1896 he was officially designated "teacher of the theory of dancing" in the St. Petersburg School of Ballet. He personally possessed a free mastery of the system of writing dance steps, and he perfected it in practice. The pupils learned dances according to the scores written by Gorsky, and Gorsky himself wrote by this method *The Sleeping Beauty* in Petipa's staging, which he put on in Moscow for two weeks. After Gorsky had transferred to work in Moscow's Bolshoi Theatre, he introduced this teaching to the Moscow Ballet School.

In 1897 Gorsky managed to publish the system in St. Petersburg with his own corrections dictated by practice ("A table of laws for the writing down of the movements of the human body, according to the system of V. I. Stepanov, artist of the St. Petersburg Ballet Theatres"), with a supplementary table of rules for writing and a key to the writing down of classical dances.

In 1899 *Examples for Reading* was published with his co-operation. In the long run, Stepanov's system was not greatly propagated because of the complicated technology of the writing (the double ciphering of the position of the human body in expansion). In the Soviet Union a series of systems of writing down dance steps was invented by such people as Sotonin, Ivanov, Maltzov, Bolotov and others, but they had no practical application.

At the present time the Methods Board of the Choreographical School of the State Academic Bolshoi Theatre of the U.S.S.R. is favourably considering a new system of writing dance steps, presented by D. Udaltzov.

APPENDIX II

Bibliography (in Russian) for the life and work of Stepanov. Information supplied by A. R. Tomsky.

1. Borisoglebsky: *Material on the History of Russian Ballet*
(Vols. I and II)
2. Works of the State Theatrical Museum of A. A. Bachruskin
M.–L. published *Iskusstvo* 1941 pp. 208–209.
Manuscript of the article of P. A. Pcelnikov
Fate of a Talented Invention
3. *Yearbook of the Imperial Theatres*, Season 1895–96
S.–P. 1896
4. **Gorsky, A. A.** *Choreography. Examples for reading* Published Imperial St. Petersburg School V.N.I. I 1899
5. Newspapers for the year 1896, St. Petersburg—
    (a) *Theatrical*. Moscow 1896 No. 54
    (b) *New Times*, No. 7147

APPENDIX III

Copy of a letter loosely inserted in some copies of Stepanov's Alphabet.

THÉATRE NATIONAL
DE
L'OPÉRA

Administration Paris, le 12 Février, 1892.
A Monsieur STÉPANOFF
Artiste des Théâtres Impériaux de
St-Petersbourg.

Monsieur,

J'ai eu l'honneur de prendre connaissance de votre nouveau traité de Chorégraphie, avec un très vif intérêt.

Je l'ai même mûrement consulté et voici mon avis à ce sujet.

Avec votre système d'anotation, je crois et j'espère que vous ferez obtenir de grands résultats.

J'applaudis à votre persévérance et aux efforts que vous avez consacrés à la réalisation de ce problême si difficile, auquel tant de Maîtres distingués se sont dévoués et consacrés à leurs tours.

J'ai la certitude, que si la nouvelle génération chorégraphique, veut s'y appliquer sagement, elle y trouvera de grandes ressources pour l'avenir dans l'art chorégraphique.

A mon tour, je tenterai à titre d'épreuve, de mettre votre système en pratique, pour ma satisfaction personelle.

Agréez, cher Monsieur Stépanoff, avec mes voeux pour le couronnement de vos efforts, l'expression de mes sentiments les plus dévoués.

J. HANSEN
MAITRE DE BALLETS
du Théâtre National de l'Opéra de Paris.

ACKNOWLEDGEMENTS

The translator wishes to thank the following for answering questions in regard to Stepanov and his system: Madame Tamara Karsavina, Madame Lydia Lopokova, Mr. A. R. Tomsky, and l'Administrateur du Théâtre National de l'Opéra, Paris.

www.ingramcontent.com/pod-product-compliance
Lightning Source LLC
Chambersburg PA
CBHW060042230426
43661CB00004B/632